SONGS
OF WALL STREET

AN ANTHOLOGY OF VERSE
FOR LITERARY INVESTORS

Written by Michael Silverstein

D0955850

RUNNING PRESS
PHILADELPHIA · LONDON

Library of Congress Cataloging-in-Publication Number 00 34989

ISBN 0-7624-0938-X
Cover and interior design by Mary Ann Liquori
Edited by Jason Rekulak and Molly Jay

This book may be ordered by mail from the publisher.
Please include $2.50 for postage and handling.
But try your bookstore first!

Running Press Book Publishers
125 South Twenty-second Street
Philadelphia, Pennsylvania 19103-4399

Visit us on the web!
www.runningpress.com

To my two best all-time friends:
Jonathan Silverstein and Kay Wood.

Contents

Introduction

Pity the poor great poets of times past. They didn't live and work during a period when the world generally and the United States in particular were experiencing the greatest stock market boom in history. And in consequence, they couldn't celebrate or castigate this extraordinary phenomenon.

This leaves the job to somebody else. More specifically, the task has fallen to me, a person with a rare combination of versifying skills (though of an admittedly derivative nature) and a knowledge of financial markets gained through labors both exhilarating and painful.

In contemplating this assignment, however, I decided that I couldn't—and indeed, shouldn't—attempt to go it alone. Why not bring in the big guns of rhyme and meter to help me with this task, I reasoned, the guys and girls that only a cruel fate had decreed would kick the bucket before they could do the job themselves.

Is it so hard, after all, to conceive of a reanimated John Donne reminding us that in a market that goes deep south, the closing bell of loss tolls for all of us? Or William Blake seeing the entire New York Stock Exchange in a single share of General Electric? Or Elizabeth Browning counting the ways she loves AOL? Or Walt Whitman, yawping with optimism, a great clear voice of a surging American Consensus on open markets? Is it so hard, in other words, to see great poets such as these going modern, versifying with the flow, jumping on a bandwagon that has today carried so many to great heights, and rolled over so many others who are less fortunate or less clever?

This book thus sets out to redress a temporal and poetic fluke. And the technique used to do this is simple: In the right column is the poet's original verse; in the left column, a contemporary market-oriented rendering of this same poem appears.

Though there's no need to read these poems in any particular order, if you choose to read this book from cover to cover, you'll find it's arranged in a rough chronological order. First come the

Elizabethans, a raunchy and opportunistic lot; followed by mystics such as Blake, religious cranks a la Goldsmith, dopers like Coleridge, and Romantics of the Wordsworth vintage; next up come the English Victorians, a marvelous collection of heroic jingoists and lost faith whiners; while the American poets who close out this book range in outlook and interests from wild optimists to tree fetishists, and include some of the poetry world's greatest show-offs (Whitman) and shut-ins (Dickinson).

Happy Reading!

MICHAEL SILVERSTEIN
PHILADELPHIA
2000

Christopher Marlowe

THE PASSIONATE
SHEPHERD TO HIS LOVE

Come live with me and be my love,
And we will all the pleasures prove,
That valleys, groves, hills and fields,
Woods and steepy mountain yields.

And we will sit upon the rocks,
Seeing the shepherds feed their flocks
By shallow rivers, to whose falls
Melodious birds sing madrigals.
And I will make thee bed of roses,
And a thousand fragrant posies,
A cap of flowers and a kirtle
Embroidered all with leaves of myrtle;

A gown made of the finest wool,
Which from our pretty lambs we pull;
Fair-lined slippers for the cold,
With buckles of the purest gold;

A belt of straw and ivy buds,
With coral clasps and amber studs;
And if these pleasures may thee move,
Come live with me and be my love.

The shepherd swains shall dance and sing
For thy delight each May morning;
If these delights they mind may move,
Then live with me and be my love.

THE PASSIONATE BROKER TO HIS CLIENT

Invest with me and be my client,
And we will all the markets troll,
For bargains and appealing yields,
In local stocks and foreign fields.

And we will take a long-term view,
Winning a bunch and losing a few
Heeding the Fed, and Abby Cohen
Knowing we need never go it alone.

And I will balance all thy holdings,
And never burden thee with scoldings;
I'll wear the dunce cap for thy failings,
Accepting blame for thy derailings;

A co-op large and mortgage-free,
You'll buy while on an earnings spree;
A closet full of minks and ermines,
A car designed by Swedes or Germans.

No more those nasty calls you'll get
Demanding payment for old debt;
And if these goodies make thee pliant,
Come trade with me and be my client.

Our research staff shall hunt and find
The treasures that will blow thy mind;
If these enrichers thy heart make pliant,
Then trade with me and be my client.

Sir Philip Sidney

DESIRE

Thou blind man's mark, thou fool's self-chosen snare,
Fond Fancy's scum and dregs of scattered thought,
Band of evils, cradle of causeless care,
Though web of will whose end is never wrought;
Desire, desire, I have too dearly bought
With price of mangled mind thy worthless ware;
Too long, too long asleep thou hast me brought,
Who should my mind to higher things prepare.
But yet in vain thou hast my ruin sought,
In vain thou mad'st me to vain things aspire,
In vain thou kindlest all thy smoky fire.
For virtue hath a better lesson taught,
Within myself to seek my only hire,
Desiring naught but how to kill desire.

RETIRE

Investment cons prey best on old age fears,
With scenes of canned cat food and roachy rooms,
Stories of illness, tales of constant cares,
Woe time for those who plan not during booms;
Retire, well-heeled, proclaim the glitzy tomes
With 'vestment schemes that make for golden years;
Too long, too long I bought this pitch 'bout doom,
And turned my back on wiser seers.
The truth is that money's no new womb,
In truth it will not kindle new life fire,
In truth it's work and friendship that inspire,
And long life without both is lengthy gloom.
So think well through your octogen desires,
So cash ain't all you leaves when you expires.

MY LOVE IS LIKE ICE

My love is like to ice, and I to fire;
How comes it then that this her cold so great
Is not dissolved through my so hot desire,
But harder grows the more I her entreat?
Or how comes it that my exceeding heat
Is not allayed by her heart frozen cold,
But that I burn much more in boiling sweat,
And feel my flames augmented manifold?
What more miraculous thing may be told,
That fire, which all things melts, should harden ice,
And ice, which is congealed with senseless cold,
Should kindle fire by wonderful device?
Such is the power of love in gentle mind,
That it can alter all the course of kind.

I NEVER THROW DICE

I never throw dice, or chance a flyer;
So how come I don't ever catch a break
In a market that keeps going higher,
And the safer I play the less my take?
Why are the picks I so carefully make
Not once arrayed near this market's crest,
And why can't I grab just one golden stake
That brings an end to my solvency quest?
Should not the aberration be confessed,
That smarts and care, old market guides, don't work,
While tips, and mindless herd runs gain the best
For stumbling into realms where profits lurk?
I spent a lifetime learning market ways,
Only to find it's buy-the-dip that pays.

William Shakespeare

SHALL I COMPARE THEE

Shall I compare thee to a Summer's day?
Thou art more lovely and more temperate:
Rough winds do shake the darling buds of May,
And Summer's lease hath all too short a date:
Sometime too hot the eye of heaven shines,
And often is his gold complexion dimm'd;
And every fair that fair sometime declines,
By chance or nature's changing course untimm'd:

But thy eternal Summer shall not fade
Nor lose possession of that fair thou ow'st;
Nor shall Death brag thou wander'st in his shade,
When in eternal lines of time thou grow'st:
So long as men can breathe, or eyes can see,
So long lives this, and this gives life to thee.

SHALL I DECLARE THEE

Shall I declare thee to the IRS?
Though cap gain piddling and so well hidden:
If I get caught it means a real mess,
And audits of other deals I've ridden:
Sometimes it's best a small gain to ignore,
When reaching for it brings unwanted heat;
Far bigger gains then exit profit's door,
As agents come thy assets to delete.

But still a gain's a thing not easy lost
And passing up a credit smacks of sin:
Each small increase to revenuers tossed,
Could better go to charity or kin:
So this I'd rather do, risk a pickle,
Than give those bastards one extra nickel.

William Shakespeare

WHO IS SILVIA?

Who is Silvia? what is she,
That all our swains commend her?
Holy, fair, and wise is she
That heaven such grace did lend her,
That she might admired be.

Is she kind as she is fair?
For beauty lives with kindness.
Love doth to her eyes repair,
To help him of his blindness,
And, being help'd, inhabits there.

Then to Silvia let us sing,
That Silvia is excelling;
She excels each mortal thing
Upon the dull earth dwelling:
To her let us garlands bring.

WHO IS BILL GATES?

Who is Bill Gates? what is he,
That analysts all commend him?
Pudgy, clever, rich is he
The market such worth does lend him,
That he might gen'rous be.

Is he wise as he is smart?
For wisdom's no computer.
Money plays a major part,
In stilling his refuters,
Who, by courts stilled, ne'er restart.

So to Bill Gates, we coo and sigh
For Microsoft's top ranking;
It keeps the tech stock index high
And other benchmarks cranking:
To him let all praises fly.

Ben Jonson

TO CELIA

Drink to me only with thine eyes,
And I will pledge with mine;
Or leave a kiss within the cup
And I'll not ask for wine.
The thirst that from the soul doth rise
Doth ask a drink divine;
But might I of Jove's nectar sup,
I would not change for thine.

I sent thee late a rosy wreath,
Not so much honoring thee
As giving it a hope that there
It could not withered be;
But thou thereon didst only breath
And sent'se it back to me;
Since when it grows, and smells, I swear
Not of itself but thee!

TO ALAN

Hint at an easing with a wink
And I will take the leap;
Or leave the benchmark rate alone
And I'll not make a peep.
In quest of truths to steer my cash
And rise above the rabble
I shun insider 'vesting tips
And heed thy delphic babble.

I sent thee late a fan mail note,
Not in jest or fun
But hoping back a letter might
With thy John Hancock come;
And even though some boilerplate
Was mailed back to me,
Since then my holdings swell, I swear
Not by themselves, but thee.

Ben Jonson

THE HOUR GLASS

Consider this small dust, here in the glass,
By atoms moved;
Could you believe that this body was
Of one that loved;
And in his mistress' flame playing like a fly,
Was turned to cinders by her eye:
Yes, and in death, as life unblessed,
To have it expressed,
Even ashes of lovers find no rest.

THE PATEK PHILIPPE

Ponder this gold watch, strapped to her wrist,
A costly toy:
A gift she'd hard earned at a late night tryst
This lady coy;
But when her nerd beau's warrants lost their zip,
The lady's love did a flip:
So, here's a lesson that's best learned
Before you get burned;
A nerd sans warrants blessed is a nerd spurned.

John Donne

DEATH BE NOT PROUD

Death be not proud, though some have called thee
Mighty and dreadful, for thou are not so;
For those whom thou think'st thou dost overthrow
Die not, poor Death; nor yet canst thou kill me.
From rest and sleep, which but thy pictures be,
Much pleasure, then from three much more must flow;
And soonest our best men with thee do go,
Rest of their bones and soul's delivery.
Thou'rt slave to fate, chance, kings, and desperate men,
And dost with poison, war, and sickness dwell;
And poppy or charms can make us sleep as well
And better than thy stroke. Why swell'st thou then?
One short sleep past, we wake eternally,
And death shall be no more; Death, thou shalt die.

DEBT'S NO DARK CLOUD

Debt's no dark cloud, though some do fear it,
Because of concern, 'bout future cash flow;
For those who see here just an undertow
See wrong, know naught, of corporate chits.
When funding growth, you must employ your wits
Take measure, so best to reap what's sown;
And best it is another's cash is blow
If ventures take a fall into the pits.
With debt enough you've left the desperate ranks
Where every change in taste and tech's a threat.
Though competition still may make you fret
Bond holders own the risk—or maybe banks.
And with some luck, you'll reach prosperity,
Then be in debt no more; Debt, you'll be history.

John Suckling

THE CONSTANT LOVER

Out upon it, I have loved
Three whole days together!
And am like to love three more,
If it prove fair weather.

Time shall moult away his wings,
Ere he shall discover
In the whole wide world again
Such a constant lover.

But in spite on't is, no praise
Is due at all to me:
Love with me had made no stays,
Had it any been but she.

Had it any been but she,
And that very face,
There had been at least ere this
A dozen dozen in her place.

THE CONSTANT LOSER

I admit it, I get spooked
Each reporting quarter!
When Amazon's earning naught,
Get a little naught-er.

Wall Street's always set a place,
For the hot air schmoozer
But it's ne'er before begot
Such a constant loser.

Who brought forth this new event?
Where should praises hover?
Know you all, his name is Jeff,
He's Time's man on the cover.

This Time's man on the cover,
Has no need for ruse,
He merely sells the credo:
E-tailing's best, the more you lose.

Robert Herrick

TO THE VIRGINS,
TO MAKE MUCH OF TIME

Gather ye rosebuds while ye may,
Old time is a still a-flying;
And this same flower that smiles today,
Tomorrow will be dying.

The glorious lamp of heaven, the sun,
The higher he's a getting,
The sooner will his race be run,
And nearer he's to setting.

That age is best which is the first,
When youth and blood are warmer;
But being spent, the worse and worst
Times still succeed the former.

Then be not coy, but use your time,
And while ye may, go marry;
For, having lost but once your prime,
You may forever tarry.

TO NEW INVESTORS, WITH SWOLLEN PORTFOLIOS

Gather ye cap gains while ye may,
When prices still are peaking;
Cause bloated markets have a way,
Of lesser levels seeking.

Inflation low, explains the game,
That's currently a–playing,
But when inflation's lost its tame,
You'll hear the pundits braying.

The going's best when yahoos hot,
For every issue slaver;
But once their fever's cooled a tot
The vultures start to gather.

So be not slow, but use this time,
While others lust for icing;
To take thy nickels turned to dimes,
And give up market dicing.

Robert Herrick

DELIGHTS IN DISORDER

A sweet disorder in the dress
Kindles in clothes a wantonness:
A lawn about the shoulders thrown
Into a fine distraction;
An erring lace, which here and there
Enthralls the crimson stomacher;
A cuff neglectful, and thereby
Ribalds to flow confusedly;
A winning wave, deserving note,
In the tempestuous petticoat;
A careless shoe-string, in whose tie
I see a wild civility,
Do more bewitch me than when art
Is too precise in every part.

PROFIT FROM CHAOS

When markets are a real mess
Big bucks are made with recklessness:
As spreads that once were small get large
It lets you practice arbitrage;
An options play, a put or call
Becomes a sudden cash windfall;
A trade on margin, oft awry
Is suddenly a genius buy;
A silly tip, you should ignore
Brings home the capital gains galore;
A deal all thought had surely died
With nifty payoffs is revived;
It's chaos, not in markets steady,
Where you make those profits heady.

NO PLATONIC LOVE

Tell me no more of minds embracing minds,
And hearts exchange'd for hearts;
That spirits spirits meet, as winds do winds,
And mix their subt'lest parts;
That two unbodied essences may kiss,
And then like Angels, twist and feel one Bliss.

I was that silly thing that once was wrought
To practice this thin love;
I climb'd from sex to soul, from soul to thought;
But thinking there to move,
Headlong I rolled from thought to soul, and then
From soul I lighted at the sex again.

As some strict down-looked men pretend to fast,
Who yet in closets eat;
So lovers who protest they spirits taste,
Feed yet on grosser meat;
I know they boast they souls to souls convey,
Howe'r they meet, the body is the way.

Come, I will undeceive thee, they that tread
Those vain aerial ways,
Are like young heirs and alchemists misled
To waste their wealth and days,
For searching thus to be forever rich,
They only find a med'cine for the itch.

HIGH COLONIC SHAM

Spare me your rap on seeking higher goals,
That money's just a way of keeping score;
That goods sold spawn goodness, that doles save souls,
And business is a bore;
That your secretive excesses loom small,
When weighed 'gainst your Feelings, your love for all.

I once did spout such princely sounding fluff
To impress those I met;
I swung 'twixt smile and guile, from soft to tough;
And to seem better yet,
Bankrolled pols who espoused these same ideals,
Then with their help closed scads of won'drous deals.

Folks nurtured when great wealth was rated ill
Such precious thinking flash;
They endlessly proclaim they've made their fill,
While scrounging for more cash;
They shout all should get a fairer shake,
But at their jobs, thy gold fillings they'd take.

Hey, enough of gray deceits, the time's come
For facing real self,
To stop pretending you're a dharma bum
Or older New Age elf,
You worship a goddess you once called bitch,
So can the sham and flaunt like super rich.

Richard Lovelace

TO LUCASTA, GOING
TO THE WARS

Tell me not, Sweet, I am unkind,
That from the nunnery
Of thy chaste breast and quiet mind
To war and arms I fly.

True, a new mistress now I chase,
The first foe in the field;
And with a stronger faith embrace
A sword, a horse, a shield.

Yet this inconstancy is such
As thou too shalt adore;
I could not love thee, Dear, so much,
Loved I not Honour more.

HONEY, I'M OFF TO THE FUTURES PITS

Cut me slack, Hon, don't be sharp-edged,
And say you'll call it quits
'Cause I've forsaken true love pledged
To haggle in the pits.

Sure, I live pork belly prices,
Pray juice and grains stay high;
Anguish 'bout each weather crisis
Too hot, too cold, too dry.

But let's be honest, lay it bare
Before you hit the door;
Though we do love each other dear,
We both love money more.

Alexander Pope

SOLITUDE (ABRIDGED)

Happy the man, whose wish and care
A few paternal acres bound,
Content to breathe his native air
In his own ground.

Whose herds with milk, whose fields with bread,
Whose flocks supply him with attire;
Whose trees in summer yield him shade,
In winter, fire.

Blest, who can unconcernedly find
Hours, days, and years slide soft away
In health of body, peace of mind;
Quiet by day.

Thus let me live, unseen, unknown;
Thus unlamented let me die,
Steal from the world, and not a stone
Tell where I lie.

HOME ALONE

Happy is she, who works at home
And her maternal chores fulfills,
Avoids the office twilight zone
And still pays bills.

Her house has heat, her car still runs,
She's satisfied with fashions staid;
Her friendships get her day time fun,
And night time, laid.

Blest, with a nonmaterial bent
No stocks, no bonds, no savings pot,
She's in good shape, makes the rent,
Smiles a lot.

She wants a life, unhooked, uncool;
From market madness, cuts all ties,
Slips through the cracks, breaks all the rules
Then ups and dies.

ON A FLY DRINKING
OUT OF HIS CUP

Busy, curious, thirsty fly!
Drink with me and drink as I:
Freely welcome to my cup,
Couldst thou sip and sip it up:
Make the most of life you may,
Life is short and wears away.

Both alike are mine and thine
Hastening quick to their decline:
Thine's a summer, mine's no more,
Though repeated to threescore.
Threescore summers, when they're gone,
Will appear as short as one!

ON A FINANCIAL ADVISOR TAKING HIS CUT

Hustling, knowing, helper dear!
Make me rich then take your share;
I begrudge you not a cut,
All of us must make our nut:
Earn a packet from your fees,
Just as long as you do please.

We are partners with joint claim
In today's great market game:
You've got clients, I'm just one.
And we'll all cry when it's done.
But for now I'll whoop, you preen,
Wallow in this pleasant dream.

Oliver Goldsmith

WOMAN

When lovely woman stoops to folly,
And finds too late that men betray,
What charm can sooth her melancholy?
What art can wash her tears away?

The only art her guilt to cover,
To hide her shame from ev'ry eye,
To give repentance to her lover,
And wring his bosom is—to die.

INTERNET INVESTOR

When young day trader stoops to folly,
  And finds the Internet betrays,
Will Cokes and donuts make him jolly?
  Will Fritos keep the tears away?

The only way his debts to cover,
And give his life the hoped for perks,
To win a smile from his mother,
And make her happy is—to work.

William Cowper

LIGHT SHINING OUT OF DARKNESS

God moves in a mysterious way,
His wonders to perform;
He plants his footsteps in the sea,
And rides upon the storm.

Deep in unfathomable mines
Of never failing skill,
He treasures up his bright designs,
And works his sovereign will.

Ye fearful saints fresh courage take;
The clouds ye so dread
Are big with mercy, and shall break
In blessings on your head.

Judge not the Lord by feeble sense,
But trust him for his grace;
Behind a frowning providence,
He hides a smiling face.

His purposes will ripen fast,
Unfolding every hour:
The bud may have a bitter taste,
But sweet will be the flower.

Blind unbelief is sure to err,
And scan his work in vain;
God is his own interpreter,
And he will make it plain.

KEEPING THE FAITH

Markets can take a torturous path,
Their purposes to achieve;
Between the sellers' fearful wrath,
And buyers fulsome greed.

But there is an Invisible Hand
That never gets it wrong,
Makes sure that things rightside do land,
Before life's closing gong.

Nay saying seers should thus back off
And stop their carping angst
Before a greater will hats doff
And ease up on their rants.

No smarts can gauge the Great Hand's ways,
You gotta just believe
That after you've traversed this maze
Good things you will receive.

In fact all questions disappear,
When looking back not front;
In retrospect all things are clear,
The past's your learning font.

So drop religion if you must,
Of politics have none;
But give the Market your blind trust,
And hope it's not a con.

Robert Burns

THE CARES O' LOVE

He
The cares o' Love are sweeter far
Than onie other pleasure;
And if sae dear its sorrows are,
Enjoyment, what a treasure!

She
I fear to try, I dare na try
As passion sae ensnaring;
For light's her heart and blithe's her song
That for nae man is caring.

THE FEARS O' LOSS

Stocks
The fears o' loss a needless care
That limits upside profit;
For if ye ne'er with stocks do dare,
Bonanza, ye'll na cop it!

Bonds
I fear the risk, it makes me twitch
When prices are not searing;
With bonds I know there's rare a glitch
And I need have na fearing.

ELEGY WRITTEN IN A COUNTRY CHURCHYARD: THE EPITAPH

Here rest his head upon the lap of Earth
A Youth to Fortune and to Fame unknown.
Fair Science frown'd not on his humble birth,
And melancholy mark'd him for her own.

Large was his bounty, and his soul sincere,
Heav'n did a recompense as largely send:
He gave to mis'ry all he had, a tear,
He gain'd from Heav'n ('twas all he wish'd) a friend.

No farther seek his merits to disclose,
Or draw his frailties from their dread abode.
There they alike in trembling hope repose,
The bosom of his Father and his God.

AN UPDATED EPITAPH

He passed away in North Miami Beach
A Lawyer who did not quite make the Grade.
Big Cases never came within his reach,
And so Big Bucks the dear man never made.

But he had savings, and some real estate,
A gen'rous market also puffed his stash:
While paying Taxes, write-offs he'd inflate,
Thus gaining near-term (his only aim) more cash.

The moral here is painful to relate,
These tactics brought The Service[1] down on heirs,
They thought they'd clear a packet after probate,
Instead got hit with paying his arrears.

[1]"The Service" is accountant-speak for the IRS

William Blake

THE NEW JERUSALEM
(ABRIDGED)

And did those feet in ancient time
Walk upon England's mountains green?
And was the holy Lamb of God
On England's pleasant pastures seen?

And did the Countenance Divine
Shine fourth upon our clouded hills?
And was Jerusalem builded here
Among these dark Satanic Mills?

Bring me my bow of burning gold!
Bring me my arrows of desire!
Bring me my spear! O clouds, unfold!
Bring me my chariot of fire!

THE NEW ECONOMY

And were not stocks in recent years
A can't–miss way to profits make?
And did not all your Market Prayers
For Nasdaq's upward progress take?

And did not Promised Recompense
Appear and pay off all your bills?
A New Economy commenced
That banished all financial ills?

Let us bring woes to carping bears!
Let us heap sorrows on their pyre!
Call your broker! Go, without fear!
Totally shun predictions dire!

William Blake

THE SCOFFERS

Mock on, mock on, Voltaire, Rousseau,
Mock on, mock on, 'tis all in vain;
You throw the sand against the wind
And the wind throws it back again.

And every sand becomes a gem
Reflected in the beams divine;
Blown back, they blind the mocker's eye,
But still in Israel's path they shine.

The atoms of Democritus
And Newton's particles of light
Are sands upon the Red Sea Shore,
Where Israel's tents do shine so bright.

THE MARKET SCOFFERS

Clamp down, clamp down, Levitt, Greenspan,
Clamp down, clamp down, it does no good;
You try to slow a raging bull
But the beast won't do as it should.

And every check becomes a goad
Repackaged in a pretty light;
Played back, it mocks all prudent pleas,
To halt its wayward frothy flight.

The scandals with derivatives,
And Hist'ry's lore of boom and bust,
Are just red flags to raging bulls,
Who leave the mockers in their dust.

Samuel Taylor Coleridge

KUBLA KHAN (ABRIDGED)

In Xanadu did Kubla Khan
A stately pleasure dome decree:
Where Alph, the sacred river ran
Through caverns measureless to man
Down to the sunless sea.
So twice five miles of fertile ground
With walls and towers were girdled round;
And there were gardens bright with sinuous rills,
Where blossomed many an incense-bearing tree;
And here were forests ancient as the hills,
Enfolding sunny spots of greenery.

But oh! that deep romantic chasm which slanted
Down the green hill athwart a cedarn cover!
A savage place! as holy and enchanted
As e'er beneath a waning moon was haunted
By woman wailing for her demon-lover!
And from this chasm, with ceaseless turmoil seething,
As if this earth in fast thick pants were breathing,
A mighty fountain momentarily was forced,
Amid whose swift half-intermitted burst
Huge fragments vaulted like rebounding hail,
Of chaffy grain beneath the thresher's flail.
And 'mid these dancing rocks at once and ever
It flung up momentarily the sacred river.
Five miles meandering with a mazy motion
Through wood and dale the sacred river ran,
Then reached the cavern measureless to man,
And sank in tumult to a lifeless ocean.
And 'mid this tumult Kubla heard from afar
Ancestral voices prophesying war!

His flashing eyes, his floating hair!
Weave a circle round him thrice,
And close your eyes with holy dread,
For he on honey-dew hath fed,
And drunk the milk of paradise.

IRWIN KAHN

In '92 did Irwin Kahn
Decide to make some big time dough:
With Al, a pal, and sister Fran
He wrote the perfect business plan
To float an IPO.
Then came five years of runnin' round
In search of capital ne'er found;
It's tough those days such funds to get
If friends and in-laws snub thy pleas,
When honest asking none begets
You end up doing Lewinskys.

But oh! from out deep wells of yearning
There suddenly appeared a trust fund bore!
A sucker angel! with no discerning
With pockets deep and little learning
Hot to show himself an entrepreneur!
And from this mating of partners ill-conceived,
This joining of chutzpah and old wealth deceived,
A mighty market miracle appeared.
With products endless, but of all profits sheared.
Great blocks of stock were quickly peddled,
And bonuses huge on the partners settled.
But under the spell of these misbegotten bosses
There came a steady stream of quarterly losses
That grew though managers got tight-fisted.
The firm's share prices slid and slid
Until there remained just asks, no bids
And the company was delisted.
And 'mid this tumult Irwin heard from a relation
Of voices prophesying litigation!

His eyes grew rheumy, his hair disheveled
He looked ahead with growing dread,
For he on lobster tails had dined,
And with Miss Utah shared a bed.

COLOGNE

In Koln,[1] a town of monks and bones,
And pavements fang'd with murderous stones,
And rags, and hags, and hideous wenches,
I counted two and seventy stenches,
All well defined, and several stinks!
Ye Nymphs that reign o'er sewers and sinks,
The river Rhine, it is well known,
Doth wash your city of Cologne;
But tell me Nymphs, what power divine
Shall henceforth wash the river Rhine?

[1]The German spelling of Cologne

WALL STREET

Wall Street, a place of cons and schemes,
And fortunes built on doctored dreams,
And fees and spreads and in-bred cronies,
I counted fifteen thousand phonies,
All MBA-ed, and oozing smarts!
The SEC patrols these parts,
With num'rous rules, it seeks to beat
White collar crime that 'fests The Street,
But really, guys, what kind of rules
Could cleanse this bustling nest of fools.

THE STAR

Twinkle, twinkle, little star,
How I wonder what you are
Up above the world so high,
Like a diamond in the sky.
Twinkle, twinkle, little star,
How I wonder what you are.

When the blazing sun is gone,
When he nothing shines upon,
Then you show your little light,
Twinkle, twinkle, all the night.
Twinkle, twinkle, little star,
How I wonder what you are.

Then the traveler in the dark
Thanks you for your tiny spark,
He could not see where to go
If you did not twinkle so.
Twinkle, twinkle, little star,
How I wonder what you are.

In the dark blue sky you keep
While you through my curtains peep,
And you never shut your eye
Till the sun is in the sky.
Twinkle, twinkle, little star,
How I wonder what you are.

THE STATION

Prattle, prattle, CNN,
Run those stock quotes by again,
Endless spouts of market news,
Spiced with brain-dead guru views,
Prattle, prattle, CNN,
Run those stock quotes by again.

When a Fed rate move comes down,
All your people race around,
Trying hard to get it right,
Prattle, prattle through the night.
Prattle, prattle, CNN,
Run those stock quotes by again.

Hooked investors bless your name
Dazzled by your guests' cheap fame,
Where would their hot money flow
If you didn't prattle so.
Prattle, prattle CNN,
Run those stock quotes by again.

From my glowing TV set,
Come the tips that wealth beget,
And I know my fortune's there
All I gotta do is stare.
Prattle, prattle, CNN,
Run that stock quote by again.

ON HIS SEVENTY-FIFTH BIRTHDAY

I strove with none, for none was worth my strife.
Nature I loved and, next to Nature, Art:
I warmed both hands before the fire of life;
It sinks, and I am ready to depart.

On Retirement At Fifty

I played the game, and sucked up with the rest.
Warrants I earned, and with these warrants, cash:
I watched the Fed and learned how to invest;
Work stinks, but I've escaped its nasty grasp.

William Wordsworth

**ON PAYING MORE ATTENTION
TO NATURAL THINGS**

THE WORLD IS TOO MUCH
WITH US; LATE AND SOON

The world is too much with us; late and soon,
Getting and spending, we lay waste all our powers;
Little we see in Nature that is ours;
We have given our hearts away, a sordid boon!
This Sea, that bares her bosom to the moon,
The winds that will be howling at all hours
And are up-gathered now like sleeping flowers;

For this, for everything, we are out of tune;
It moves us not, Great God! I'd rather be
A Pagan suckled in a creed outworn;
So might I, standing on this pleasant lea,
Have glimpses that would make me less forlorn;
Have sight of Proteus rising from the sea,
Or hear old Triton blow his wreathed horn.

GLOBALIZATION'S COMING; TOO DAMN FAST

Globalization's coming; too damn fast,
Everything's for sale, no one's in control;
Old traditions no longer have a role;
The damage done to land and air, it's truly vast!
Into the world's waters we've foulness cast,
The clearing of great forests are the tolls,
Ignored by those pursuing profit's goals.

Nothing much counts, it seems, but bottom lines;
The only fear—a no Big Bonus year!
Even one suckled on Wall Street Journal screeds
Like myself, fin'ly can no longer cheer
The cost to nature that global growth breeds;
We've learned that mindless worship of bull and bear
Taken too far provokes unseemly deeds.

William Wordsworth

COMPOSED UPON WESTMINSTER BRIDGE (SEPTEMBER 3, 1802)

Earth has not anything to show more fair:
Dull would he be of soul who could pass by
A sight so touching in its majesty:
This City now doth, like a garment, wear
The beauty of the morning: silent, bare,
Ships, towers, domes, theaters, and temples lie
Open unto the fields, and to the sky;
All bright and glittering in the smokeless air.
Never did sun more beautifully steep
In his first splendor, valley, rock, or hill;
Ne'er saw I, never felt, a calm so deep!
The river glideth at his own sweet will:
Dear God! the very houses seem asleep;
And all that mighty heart is lying still!

COMPOSED WHEN THE NASDAQ FIRST HIT 5,000
(MARCH 7, 2000)

No market has ever risen so fast:
Only the cautious did miss their big chance
To hop a ride on this bubble flyer:
Nasdaq triumphs, all its critics, aghast
Fell silent this morning, devoid of rant,
Dot.coms and bio-techs, all found buyers
And what once sold high, now sells much higher;
All now agree, all worries here are past.
And no analyst does raise a peep
As this splendid ascent reaches its peak;
For from price jumps here they income reap!
So it pays no nasty comment to speak:
Surely! We'll all never rise from our sleep;
And find this great ark has done sprung a leak!

SHE WALKS IN BEAUTY
LIKE THE NIGHT

She walks in beauty, like the night
Of cloudless climes and starry skies;
And all that's best of dark and bright
Meet in her aspect and her eyes:
Thus mellowed to that tender light
Which heaven to gaudy day denies.

One shade the more, one ray the less,
Had half impaired the nameless grace
Which waves in every raven tress,
Or softly lightens o'er her face;
Where thoughts serenely sweet express
How pure, how dear their dwelling-place.

And on that cheek, and o'er that brow,
So soft, so calm, yet eloquent,
The smiles that win, the tints that glow,
But tell of days in goodness spent,
A mind at peace with all below,
A heart whose love is innocent!

SHE WALKS TO WORK AT GOLDMAN SACHS

She walks to work, at Goldman Sachs
At crack of dawn each bus'ness day,
And all the praise put out by flacks
About her marv'lous market play
Seems tepid 'gainst the simple facts
That what she picks gets up and quacks.

One option more, one future less,
Would make this guru seem unfit
And raise a cry of great distress,
Among the clients who take the hit;
But she with Streetwise insights blessed
By market slides in never bit.

And from those lips, and out that mouth
Come soothing words so soft and purry,
Of deals that rise and ne'er go south
And risks for which you're never sorry;
A face devoid of frowns and pouts,
A voice that coos: What me worry?

John Keats

ON FIRST LOOKING INTO CHAPMAN'S HOMER

Much have I travel'd in the realms of gold,
And many goodly states and kingdoms seen;
Round many western islands have I been
Which bards in fealty to Apollo hold.
Oft of one wide expanse have I been told
That deep-brow'd Homer ruled as his demesne;
Yet did I never breathe its pure serene
Till I heard Chapman speak out loud and bold:
Then felt I like some watcher of the skies
When a new planet swims into his ken;
Or like stout Cortez when with eagle eyes
He star'd at the Pacific—and all his men
Look'd at each other with a wild surmise—
Silent upon a peak in Darien.

ON FIRST HEARING OF THE WORLD BANK'S BONERS

Long I've dabbl'd in money's higher realm,
Where bad loans and bad politics commune;
Seen good intentions turn to shambl'd ruin
In lands where thugs the law do overwhelm.
Often I've thought that things could not get worse
That the dumbest boners had all been made;
Then I came upon a shameful glade
The garden funded by the World Bank's purse:
I felt as if I'd stumbled on a plain
Where seed corn grows to wheat and acorns pine;
Or like young Alice in a rabbit's wake
Fell down a bad trip hole—where hatters dine
And potions that cause all to undertake—
Madly self and others to redefine.

John Keats

When I Have Fears That I May Cease To Be

When I have fears that I may cease to be
Before my pen has gleaned my teeming brain,
Before high piled books, in charact'ry,
Hold like rich garners the full-ripened grain;
When I behold, upon the night's starred face,
Huge cloudy symbols of a high romance,
And think that I may never live to trace
Their shadows, with the magic hand of chance;
And when I feel, fair creature of an hour!
That I shall never look upon thee more,
Never have relish in the faery power
Of unreflecting love!—then on the shore
Of the wide world I stand alone, and think
Till love and fame to nothingness do sink.

WHEN I HAVE FEARS
THAT I MAY LOSE MY STASH

When I have fears that I may lose my stash
Before tasting all things that money buys,
And wander the world, without ready cash,
Reduced to eating burgers and french fries;
I have been forced to face one painful fact,
That the power brokers of high finance,
Can without ever caring, trash my act
Leaving me broke, while they start a new dance;
When I have felt thus hopelessly possessed,
I've sometimes been by nasty anger bossed,
Turning a home-life that long was much blessed
Into a home-life stressed—its love outsourced.
So now again I've reassessed, and thinks
A life sans love—like one sans money—stinks.

OZYMANDIAS

I met a traveler from an antique land
Who said: Two vast and trunkless legs of stone
Stand in the desert. Near them, on the sand,
Half sunk, a shattered visage lies, whose frown,
And wrinkled lip, and sneer of cold command,
Tell that its sculptor well these passions read,
Which yet survive, stamped on these lifeless things,
The hand that mocked them and the heart that fed;
And on the pedestal these words appear:
"My name of Ozymandias, king of kings:
Look upon my works, ye Mighty, and despair."
Nothing beside remains. Round the decay
Of that colossal wreck, boundless and bare
The lone and level sands stretch far away.

BRADYMANDIAS[1]

I met an owner of emerging market debt
Who said: A trough of bonds, defaulted or arreared
Clutter portfolios. Beside them, a paper trail lies,
Yellowed and torn, the remnant commentaries
Of financial scribes, assigned the puff piece beat,
Who praised in bold, but sneered between the lines,
Catching well the arrogant self-regard and certitude
Of those who do good with other people's coin.
And under a Treasury official's picture these words were writ:
"I am Bradymandias, lender of lender:
Look upon My work, ye private issuers, and despair!"
All around, there's nothing else in view
But a neat stack of IOUs, browning and sterile
The faded record of economies withering to the horizon.

[1]Brady bonds, named after a former U.S. Treasury Secretary, seek to reduce
the debt burden of emerging nations by backing this debt with U.S. Treasuries.

MUSIC, WHEN SOFT VOICES DIE

Music, when soft voices die,
Vibrates in the memory.
Odours, when sweet violets sicken,
Live within the sense they quicken.

Rose leaves, when the rose is dead,
Are heap'd for the beloved's bed;
And so thy thoughts when thou art gone,
Love itself shall slumber on.

MERGERS, THAT WILL NEVER FLY

Mergers, that will never fly,
Their sponsors cunning belie.
Buyouts, by leverage floated,
Often later get you goated.

Earnings, less than what was said,
Will make an analyst see red.
Beware of things that can go wrong
Long before you ventures spawn.

Sir Walter Scott

INNOMINATUS

Breathes there a man with soul so dead,
Who never to himself hath said,
"This is my own, my native land!"
Whose heart hath ne'er within him burn'd
As home his footsteps he hath turn'd
From wandering on a foreign strand?
If such there breathe, go, mark him well;
For him no Minstrel raptures swell;
High though his titles, proud his name,
Boundless his wealth as wish can claim;
Despite these titles, power and pelf,
The wretch, concentred all in self,
Living, shall forfeit all renown,
And, doubly dying, shall go down
To the vile dust from whence he sprung,
Unwept, unhonour'd, and unsung.

INGRATICUS

Show me a guy who's gone so fey,
When money beckons, he won't say,
"Gimme some more, I like the stuff!"
When markets open every morn
I feel myself again reborn
And love to play it hard and tough.
If this guy's found, steer clear his fate;
No piece in Barrons will he rate;
Calm though his spirit, quiet his days,
Disdaining wealth and other's praise;
He's missed this era's premier nexus
And never even owned a Lexus,
Alive, he'll not atop wealth sit,
And dead, he'll get no Times obit,
This old econ'my reprobate,
Unwired, unleveraged, out-of-date.

Leigh Hunt

JENNY KISS'D ME

Jenny kiss'd me when we met,
Jumping from the chair she sat in;
Time, you thief, who love to get
Sweets into your list, put that in!
Say I'm weary, say I'm sad,
Say that health and wealth have miss'd me,
Say I'm growing old, but add,
Jenny kiss'd me.

GREENSPAN STIFF'D ME

Greenspan stiff'd me when he set,
Int'rest rates at levels higher;
Gad, what grief, such hikes beget
For ev'ry would-be home buyer!
Say that owning's just a fad,
Say no mortgage debt will haunt me,
Say my rental's nice, but add,
Greenspan stiff'd me.

John Clare

WRITTEN IN NORTHAMPTON COUNTY ASYLUM

I am! yet what I am who cares, or knows?
My friends forsake me like a memory lost.
I am the self-consumer of my woes;
They rise and vanish, an obvious host,
Shadows of life, whose very soul is lost.
And yet I am—I live—though I am toss'd.

Into the nothingness of scorn and noise,
Into the living sea of waking dream,
Where there is neither sense of life, nor joys,
But the huge shipwreck of my own esteem
And all that's dear. Even those I loved the best
Are strange—nay, they are stranger than the rest.

I long for scenes where man has never trod,
For scenes where woman never smiled or wept,
There to abide with my Creator, God,
And sleep as I in childhood sweetly slept,
Full of high thoughts, unborn. So let me die,
The grass below; above, the vaulted sky.

SMITTEN AT A HAMPTONS, L.I. LAWN PARTY

She's here! she seems alone, but should I speak?
My friends assure me I don't stand a chance.
I ooze neurosis, and my chin is weak.
She'll see these defects, and dispatch a lance,
Unman me there, with just a single glance,
And so I'll stand, alive, but wet of pants.

Why dare this recklessness, and all it bodes,
With a hot tech analyst on a roll,
A wired woman who knows The Street, its codes,
How could she fall for a back office mole
With yearly bonus small? Yet I feel drawn
By visions—half professional, half porn.

I want a life by lots of money fueled,
To bed someone who always makes big deals,
A woman in Investment Banking, Schooled,
Who doesn't snore and buys me fancy meals,
Has deep thoughts like all good money minters,
We'll beach here summers, Manhattan winters.

Edward Fitzgerald

The Rubaiyat of Omar Khayyam (Excerpts)

Come, fill the Cup, and in the fire of Spring
Your winter garment of Repentance fling:
Thy Bird of Time has but a little way
To flutter—and the Bird is on the Wing.

* * * * * * * *

A Book of Verses underneath the Bough,
A Jug of Wine, a Loaf of Bread—and Thou
Beside me singing in the Wilderness—
Oh, Wilderness were Paradise enow.

* * * * * * *

Some for the Glories of This World; and some
Sigh for the Prophet's Paradise to come;
Ah, take the Cash, and let the Credit go,
Nor heed the rumble of a distant Drum!

OMAR'S RUBIETTES (EXCERPTS)

Come, buy some stock, and take a little flyer
That boosts your pension equity still higher.
The end of dreary work and stressed out days
Now beckons—and the market's still a'fire.

* * * * * * *

Irrational exuberance propping up the Dow,
A pliant SEC, a helpful Fed—and wow!
Rejoice and welcome the new paradigm—
This paradigm is Paradise renamed.

* * * * * * *

Some focus on the near-term dips; and some
To macro fears succumb,
Ah, spend thy cash and live on credit flow
Nor fear the gloom and doom to come!

BREAK, BREAK, BREAK

Break, break, break,
On thy cold gray stones, O Sea!
And I would that my tongue could utter
The thoughts that arise in me.

O, well for the fisherman's boy,
That he shouts with his sister at play!
O, well for the sailor lad,
That he sings in his boat on the bay!

And the stately ships go on
To their haven under the hill;
But O for the touch of a vanish'd hand,
And the sound of a voice that is still!

Break, break, break,
At the foot of they crags, O Sea!
But the tender grace of a day that is dead
Will never come back to me.

RAKE, RAKE, RAKE

Rake, rake, rake,
All your market gains, Not Me!
For I just stand and curse and mutter
At all this transient glee.

Yes, it's great for entrepreneurs,
Who can follow their dreams to great ends!
Yes, it's great for working Joes,
Whose retirement funds it extends!

Big capital conquers all
Its naysayers mostly are still;
But 'Fie on that harsh Invisible Hand,
I spout my Marxist rhetoric still!

Rake, rake, rake,
You free market lovers, Not Me!
For from the safety of my long tenured perch
I can reality flee.

THE CHARGE OF THE LIGHT BRIGADE (ABRIDGED)

I

Half a league, half a league,
Half a league onward,
All in the valley of Death
Rode the six hundred.
"Forward the Light Brigade!
Charge for the guns!" he said.
Into the valley of Death
Rode the six hundred.

II

"Forward the Light Brigade!"
Was there a man dismay'd?
Not tho' the soldiers knew
Someone had blunder'd.
Theirs not to make reply,
Theirs not to reason why,
Theirs but to do and die.
Into the valley of Death
Rode the six hundred.

III

Cannon to right of them,
Cannon to left of them,
Cannon in front of them
Volley'd and thunder'd;
Storm'd at with shot and shell,
Boldly they rode and well
Into the jaws of Death,
Into the mouth of hell
Rode the six hundred.

IV

When can their glory fade?
O the wild charge they made!
All the world wonder'd.
Honor the charge they made!
Honor the Light Brigade,
Noble six hundred!

THE PLIGHT OF THE CHARGE BRIGADE

I

Charge it up, charge it up,
Charge up that purchase,
Deep in the valley of Debt
Plunge the card holders.
Stuff they don't really need!
Charge for the fun—their creed.
Into the valley of Debt
Plunge the card holders.

II

Stuff they don't really need!
Why should they be afraid?
Their stocks are doing well
They figure what the hell.
No stops to reason why
Just buy until you die,
Into the valley of Debt
Plunge the card holders.

III

Soft goods in front of them,
Hard goods in back of them,
Goods on all sides of them
Goods without number;
Rush through the big mall store,
Scope out its sales floor,
Into the jaws of Debt,
Into the Land of More
Plunge the card holders.

IV

Why should this frenzy stop?
O what great stuff they got!
All the world marvels.
Honor the charge brigade!
Forget the int'rest paid,
Happy card holders!

THE LATEST DECALOGUE

Thou shall have one God only; who
Would be at the expense of two?
No graven images may be
Worshipped, except the currency:
Swear not at all; for, for thy curse
Thine enemy is none the worse:
At church on Sunday to attend
Will serve to keep the world thy friend:
Honour thy parents that is, all
From whom advancement may befall:
Thou shalt not kill; but needs't not strive
Officiously to keep alive:
Do not adultery commit;
Advantage rarely comes of it:
Thou shalt not steal; an empty feat,
When it's so lucrative to cheat:
Bear not false witness; let the lie
Have time on its own wings to fly:
Thou shalt not covet, but tradition
Approves all forms of competition.

THE TEN MARKET COMMANDMENTS

When your bum deals rise from the muck
Thank Higher Powers, never luck;
Win foreign contracts with bribes paid
Then shout hosannas to Free Trade;
Return not slights, it makes things worse
Trim down instead the slighter's purse;
Never hide your civic virtues
Hype them in TV commercials;
Mom and dad, for your biog, props
Buy mom a condo, dad new socks;
Destroy no one, as you ascend
Unless, of course, it serves some end;
Dipping pens in office inkwells
Often has sad courtroom sequels;
Don't bother stealing, it's passe
Peddling bonds is the better way;
Disdain lying to those you've bled
Send them to your lawyer instead;
Covet all, but then reveal
Your actions serve the public weal.

Arthur Hugh Clough

SAY NOT THE STRUGGLE (ABRIDGED)

Say not the struggle naught availeth,
The labour and the wounds are vain,
The enemy faints not, nor faileth,
And as things have been they remain.

If hopes were dupes, fears may be liars;
It may be, in yon smoke conceal'd,
Your comrades chase e'en now the fliers,
And, but for you, possess the field.

For while the tired waves, vainly breaking,
Seem here no painful inch to gain,
Far back, through creeks and inlets making,
Comes silent, flooding in the main.

And not by eastern windows only,
When daylight comes, comes in the light;
In front the sun climbs slow, how slowly!
But westward look, the land is bright!

SAY NOT YOUR GOLD FUND

Say not your gold fund naught a'groweth,
It lies there like a lump of lead,
Nor does it dividends off throweth,
Indeed, it looketh to be dead.

If shares are down, demand may be quick'ning;
It may be, in markets still conceal'd,
Gold buyers bounce from losses sick'ning,
And, hid from you, renew their zeal.

For while inflation, wildly racing,
Now seems a distant set of spikes,
Big banks, liquidity embracing
Seem headed down this same old pike.

So not by this day's price quote only,
When planning trades, and setting goals;
The current state of gold is lowly,
But meltdowns come, and up she goes!

DOVER BEACH (ABRIDGED)

The sea is calm tonight,
The tide is full, the moon lies fair
Upon the straits; on the French coast the light
Gleams and is gone; the cliffs of England stand,
Glimmering and vast, out in the tranquil bay.
Come to the window, sweet is the night air!
Only, from the long line of spray
Where the sea meets the moon-blanched land,
Listen! you hear the grating roar
Of pebbles which the waves draw back, and fling,
At their return, up the high strand,
Begin, and cease, and then again begin,
With tremulous cadence slow, and bring
The eternal note of sadness in.

Ah, love, let us be true
To one another! for the world, which seems
To lie before us like a land of dreams,
So various, so beautiful, so new,
Hath really neither joy, nor love, nor light,
Nor certitude, nor peace, nor help for pain;
And we are here as on a darkling plain,
Swept with confused alarms of struggle and flight,
Where ignorant armies clash by night.

OVER REACH

There's no alarm tonight,
The news is good, the Dow is not
In nasty straits; on France's bourse no blight
Drags prices down, and London's own exchange,
Bumbling and crass, mopes on its laggard way.
Boot up your laptop, check out what is hot!
Only, as you prune the decay
In stocks across sector ranges
Look close! see how they bounce about
Like baseballs that investors clutch, then fling.
Their prices sway, they madly change,
Ascend to cheers, and then collapse like stones
In volatile bungee dives, which bring
The horrible fear of losses home.

Ah, greed, let us not take
This shit to heart! for markets, which seem
To offer hope with countless make-wealth schemes,
Sans new-learning, sans brain-straining, sans shakes,
Hath no gift that's sure, nor fast, nor safe,
No guarantees, no dunks, no fail-proof nets;
You jump in and caress your paper bets,
Caught up in rumors of maybe and might,
While faceless bettors shape your plight.

THE LOST CHORD

Seated one day at the Organ,
I was weary and ill at ease,
And my fingers wandered idly
Over the noisy keys.

I do not know what I was playing,
Or what I was dreaming then;
But I struck one chord of music,
Like the sound of a great Amen.
It flooded the crimson twilight,
Like the close of an Angel's Psalm,
And it lay on my fevered spirit
With a touch of infinite calm.

It quieted pain and sorrow,
Like love overcoming strife;
It seemed the harmonious echo
From our discordant life.

It linked all perplexed meanings
Into one perfect peace,
And trembled away into silence
As if it were loath to cease.

I have sought, but I seek it vainly,
That one lost chord divine,
Which came from the soul of the Organ,
And entered into mine.

It may be that Death's bright angel
Will speak in that chord again,—
It may be that only in Heaven
I shall hear that grand Amen.

THE LOST HOARD

One day while playing the market,
I was snorting a line of blow,
When up popped on my desktop screen
Stock names I didn't know.

I had no idea who sent them,
Or why they came at this time;
But wired as I was just then
I figured it must be a Sign.
The screen seemed aglow with promise,
It looked like a Portent Divine,
In a fever I dialed my broker
And invested my last dime.

A wond'rous calm possessed me,
Sweet certainty filled my mind;
I had a luxurious vision,
The high six figure kind.

The vision's clear dazzling outlines
Defined a perfect whole,
Its clarity made me feel certain
I was fin'ly on a roll.

Then it hit, the big double whammy,
That made me lose my cool,
First my stocks went into the Toilet,
Then my screen read "April Fool."

One day I might meet the jokester
Whose tip sent me into the ditch,
And though I'm more lover than fighter
I'll kill that son of a bitch.

Elizabeth Barrett Browning

HOW DO I LOVE THEE?

How do I love thee? Let me count the ways.
I love thee to the depth and breadth and height
My soul can reach, when feeling out of sight
For the ends of Being and ideal Grace.
I love thee to the level of everyday's
Most quiet need, by sun and candle-light.
I love thee freely, as men strive for Right;
I love thee purely, as they turn from Praise.
I love thee with the passion put to use
In my old griefs, and with my childhood's faith.
I love thee with a love I seemed to lose
With my lost saints. I love thee with the breath,
Smiles, tears, of all my life!—and, if God choose,
I shall but love thee better after death.

WHERE WENT MY MONEY?

Where went my money? Therein lies a tale.
I lost it in the slip and skip and lurch
That stocks can take, when traders go in search
Of phantom market Peaks and endless Tops.
I lost it in the everyday churning gale
Of brokers' fees, and other Wall Street perks.
I lost it quickly, hot to buy on dips;
I lost it slowly, taking guru tips.
I lost it with a frenzy once reserved
For sporting teams, and raunchy teenage dreams.
I lost it in a way that never swerved
From dumb old paths—But now with plans more sound
Cool, calm, rearing to go!—and, fresh Reserves,
I know I'll do much better this time 'round.

Robert Browning

MEETING AT NIGHT

The gray sea and the long black land;
And the yellow half-moon large and low;
And the startled little waves that leap
In fiery ringlets from their sleep,
As I gain the cove with pushing prow,
And quench its speed in the slushy sand.

Then a mile of warm sea-scented beach;
Three fields to cross till a farm appears;
A tap on the pane, the quick sharp scratch
And the blue spurt of a lighted match.
And a voice less loud, through its joys and fears,
Then the two hearts beating each to each!

DOING THE DEAL

The staid old firm had rich cash flows;
With an entrenched old-boy board in charge;
A tender offer[1] put it in play
Which the board tried hard to keep at bay,
A poison pill[2] was the chosen dodge,
And it seemed like we might come to blows.

So we hard-haggled to close the breech;
In ways that spruced up all our careers;
The board would back down, its nays go mute
And we'd give out gold parachutes,
The market approved, giving three loud cheers
As we deal-makers smiled, leech to leech!

[1]Announcement by one company that it plans to buy
shares of another company, usually as part of a takeover

[2]A mechanism involving convertible bonds
designed to frustrate a takeover attempt

Robert Browning

PIPPA'S SONG

The year's at the spring,
And day's at the morn;
Morning's at seven;
The hillside's dew-pearl'd;
The larks on the wing;
The snails on the thorn;
God's in His heaven;
All's right with the world!

PROZAC'S SONG

It's time for a fling,
The boom's at its dawn;
Nasdaq is soaring;
Investors cash-bless'd;
The stocks all have zing;
The bonds int'rest spawn;
Mammon's a'roaring—
All dance to his jest!

Christina Rossetti

WHEN I AM DEAD,
MY DEAREST

When I am dead, my dearest,
Sing no sad songs for me;
Plant thou no roses at my head,
Nor shady cypress tree:
Be the green grass above me
With showers and dewdrops wet;
And if thou wilt, remember,
And if thou wilt, forget.

I shall not see the shadows,
I shall not feel the rain;
I shall not hear the nightingale
Sing on, as if in pain;
And dreaming through the twilight
That doth not rise nor set,
Haply I may remember,
And haply may forget.

WHAT I MOST DREAD, DEAR CLIENT

What I most dread, dear client,
Is that you will depart;
And find you do not need my help,
The wisdom I impart:
Stay calm with no advisor
When markets go chug-chug;
And if you win, be happy,
And if you lose, just shrug.

I shan't then get commissions,
I shan't then get my fees;
I shan't then buy a Hampton house
My trophy wife, to please;
So stick with your obsessions
To squeeze dry ev'ry bet,
And whether end you rich or poor
My own goals will be met.

Dante Gabriel Rossetti

THE WOODSPURGE

The wind flapped loose, the wind was still,
Shaken out dead from tree and hill;
I had walked on at the wind's will;
I sat now, for the wind was still.

Between my knees my forehead was,
My lips drawn in, said not Alas!
My hair was over in the grass,
My naked ears heard the day pass.

My eyes, wide open, had the run
Of some ten weeds to fix upon;
Among these few, out of the sun,
The woodspurge flowered, three cups in one.

From perfect grief there need not be
Wisdom or even memory;
One thing then learned remains with me:
The woodspurge has a cup of three.

THE WIND FARM SPLURGE

To save the earth, and keep it pure,
Without myself becoming poor,
I found a stock with glitz galore,
A wind farm deal I thought would soar.

My heart told me this deal was green
With Nature's Breath it pumped juice clean!
From nasty nukes it would us wean
And I would hefty profits glean.

Now brokers statements have arrived,
They show a tough year I've survived;
But one bad bet, by heart advised,
My wind farm splurge can't be revived.

Sometimes you gotta take a whack
To get your thinking back on track;
The lesson here's not hard to crack:
Not all that goes around comes back.

INVICTUS

Out of the night that covers me,
Black as the Pit from pole to pole,
I thank whatever gods may be
For my unconquerable soul.

In the fell clutch of circumstance
I have not winced nor cried aloud.
Under the bludgeoning of chance
My head is bloody, but unbowed.

Beyond this place of wrath and tears
Looms but the horror of the shade,
And yet the menace of the years
Finds, and shall find me, unafraid.

It matters not how strait the gate,
How charged with punishments the scroll,
I am the master of my fate,
I am the captain of my soul.

CONVICTUS

Out of the hands of the SEC,
Back from the Pit where the felons board,
I thank the lawyers who earned their fees
For my undiminished hoard.

Caught in the grip of nasty fate
I opted for a nolo shot.
Under the laws of New York State
I did some time, but not a lot.

Beyond the cell, the bars, the wire
Looms a record I'll always bear,
Yet aided by a p.r. choir
A brighter image will soon appear.

It's not important the stuff I did,
How crookedly I played the game,
I can buy out of a blighted past,
I am above a sense of shame.

Algernon Charles Swinburne

BEFORE THE BEGINNING OF YEARS (ABRIDGED)

Before the beginning of years
There came to the making of man
Time, with a gift of tears;
Grief, with a glass than ran;
Pleasure, with pain for leaven;
Summer, with flowers that fell;
Remembrance fallen from heaven,
And madness risen from hell;
Strength without hands to smite;
Love that endures for a breath;
Night, the shadow of light,
And life, the shadow of death.

And the high gods took in hand
Fire, and the falling of tears,
And a measure of sliding sand
From under the feet of the years;
With travail and heavy sorrow,
The holy spirit of man.
They breathed upon his mouth.
They filled his body with life;
With his lips he travaileth;
In his heart is a blind desire,
In his eyes foreknowledge of death;
He weaves, and is clothed in derision;
Sows, and he shall not reap;
His life is a watch and a vision
Between a sleep and a sleep.

BEFORE THE OPENING GONG

Before the opening gong
There came to a new trading day
News, of dips in Hong Kong;
Fears, a bond might not pay;
Profits, that came with a warning;
Earnings, but sales that fell;
Inflation, again a–spawning,
And rate hikes that make debtors yell;
Firms crying out for new funds;
Deals that fall through the cracks;
A press rife with bad puns,
Whose pages are filled by hacks.

Then central banks took their stand
Meeting, they jointly declared,
That the markets shall softly land
And good times will not be impaired;
They opened wide their vaults,
And out gushed a sea of cash
Which checked fears of defaults
And gave new life to the bash,
But down deep grew seeds of doubt
Investors, turned more fretful;
Their hands still reached to acquire,
But their heads saw downturns dreadful;
They whine, 'cause of stock dilutions;
Beg, but their power's gone mute;
Searching in vain for solutions
Between law suit and law suit.

HAP

If but some vengeful god would call to me
From up the sky, and laugh: "Thou suffering thing,
Know that thy sorrow is my ecstasy,
That thy love's loss is my hate's profiting!"
Then would I bear it, clench myself, and die,
Steeled by the sense of ire unmerited;
Half-eased in that a Powerfuller than I
Had willed and meted me the tears I shed.

But not so. How arrives it joy lies slain,
And why unblooms the best hope ever sown?
Crass causality obstructs the sun and rain,
And dicing Time for gladness casts a moan.
These purblind Doomsters had as readily strewn
Blisses about my pilgrimage as pain.

PAP

If guys with inside dope would ring me up
On cell phones sleek, and boast: "Poor out-the-loop fool,
Your wrong side trading is my winner's cup,
Those off-mark bets, my daughter's private school!"

Then could I hack it, eat the pain, jog free,
Hardened to a life of chump change well deserved;
Chill out calm that one far wilier than me
Had proven sharper brained and better nerved.

But t'aint so. How come profit flees my grasp
And why plummets all my can't-miss picks?
Wild volatility leaves me here to gasp
At mindless swings of markets shaped by hicks.
These puckish Dabblers out for trading kicks
Dumbly burden me down with losses vast.

REQUIEM

Under the wide and starry sky
Dig the grave and let me lie:
Glad did I live and gladly die,
And I laid me down with a will.

This be the verse you grave for me:
Here he lies where he long'd to be;
Home is the sailor, home from the sea,
And the hunter home from the hill.

CHAPTER 11

Debtor I come to bankrupt court
Where the lawyers love to sport:
Once it was me their talents bought,
But now I get barbed by their skills.

These are the laws they say I spurned:
I spent more than I ever earned;
Stuck it to others, they got burned,
Now payback is due on my bills.

Robert Louis Stevenson

HAPPY THOUGHT

The world is so full of a number of things,
I'm sure we should all be as happy as kings.

WHAT WE'RE TAUGHT

Investing's a cinch and unless we muff it,
We'll all end up rich as old Warren Buffet.

Francis William Bourdillon

THE NIGHT HAS A THOUSAND EYES

The night has a thousand eyes,
And the day but one;
Yet the light of the bright world dies
With the dying sun.

The mind has a thousand eyes,
And the heart but one;
Yet the light of a whole life dies
When love is done.

EACH DAY BRINGS
A THOUSAND LIES

Each day brings a thousand lies,
And a few grains of truth;
But we opt for the former with sighs
'Cause our nerves it soothes.

Good times bring the happy lies,
No one wants to doubt;
And all at once wealth flies
Then comes the rout.

WOODMAN, SPARE THAT TREE (ABRIDGED)

Woodman, spare that tree!
Touch not a single bough!
In youth it sheltered me,
And I'll protect it now.

'Twas my forefather's hand
That placed it near his cot;
There, woodman, let it stand,
Thy ax shall harm it not!

Woodman, forbear thy stroke!
Cut not its earthbound ties!
Oh! spare that aged oak,
Now towering to the skies.

When but an idle boy
I sought its grateful shade;
In all their gushing joy
Here, too, my sisters played.

My mother kissed me here,
My father pressed my hand;
Forgive this foolish tear,
But let that old oak stand!

Old tree, the storm still brave!
And, woodman, leave the spot!
While I've a hand to save,
Thy ax shall harm it not.

FASB, CHANGE NO REGS!

FASB[1], change no regs!
Squeeze not our bottom line!
Freedom gives markets legs,
More rules make them decline.

'Twas long benign neglect
That let our stock price soar;
FASB, don't cause a wreck,
With regs that make us poor.

FASB, pooling's[2] O.K!
Accounting for goodwill's dumb!
Please! don't make us pay
Now that we're having such fun.

Whenever we sold shares
A Big 5 firm dropped by;
They've backed our claims for years,
You know they'd never lie.

Investors love our pitch
The press has played its part;
Why should a ruling switch
Upset this applecart!

You know to pols we give!
And, FASB, they give back!
So let's play live let live,
And you cut us some slack.

[1]Financial Accounting Standards Board, which helps decide how material found in financial documents like annual reports must be presented

[2]Pooling is a technique that can make the bottom line of a newly merged company look better by eliminating the necessity of figuring in goodwill–payment made in excess of a company's book value.

EXCELSIOR (ABRIDGED)

The shades of night were falling fast,
And through an Alpine village passed
A youth, who bore, 'mid snow and ice,
A banner with the strange device,
Excelsior!

His brow was sad; his eyes beneath,
Flashed like a falchion from its sheath,
And like a silver clarion rung
The accents of that unknown tongue,
Excelsior!

"Try not the pass!" the old man said;
"Dark lowers the tempest overhead,
The roaring torrent is deep and wide!"
And loud that clarion voice replied,
Excelsior!

"Oh stay," the maiden said, "and rest
Thy weary head upon this breast!"
A tear stood in his bright blue eye,
But still he answered, with a sigh,
Excelsior!

A traveler, by the faithful hound,
Half-buried in the snow was found,
Still grasping in his hand of ice
That banner with the strange device,
Excelsior!

There in the twilight cold and gray,
Lifeless, but beautiful, he lay,
And from the sky, serene and far,
A voice fell, like a falling star,
Excelsior!

ALKA-SELTZER

———

The closing bell was drawing near,
And with it came a touch of fear,
Young Ed, who trades throughout the day,
Sensed soon there would be hell to pay,
Alka-Seltzer!

His mouth gone dry, his eyes transfixed,
A desk computer flashed his picks,
It showed he'd acted much too bold
He'd overbought and undersold,
Alka-Seltzer!

"Don't be a schmuck," an old hand warned;
"Big losses are by big risk spawned,
Build slow your pile, don't lose control!"
But Ed thought he was on a roll,
Alka-Seltzer!

"Ease up," his wife advised, "be cool
Don't blow our winnings like a fool!"
Ed heard her 'plaint and felt the goad,
Alas be'd frozen on this road,
Alka-Seltzer!

Some weeks later, a friend of Ed,
At mid-day found him in his bed,
His face unshaved, his breath a'fire
He clutched a broker's statement dire,
Alka-Seltzer!

Ed's left the game that made him throb,
He's focused, full-time, on his job,
But new investors have the itch,
Quite sure their stocks will make them rich,
Alka-Seltzer!

THE ARROW AND THE SONG

I shot an arrow into the air,
It fell to earth, I knew not where;
For, so swiftly it flew, that sight
Could not follow it in its flight.

I breathed a song into the air,
It fell to earth, I knew not where;
For who has sight so keen and strong,
That it can follow the flight of song?

Long, long afterward, in an oak
I found the arrow, still unbroken;
And the song, from beginning to end,
I found again in the heart of a friend.

THE BROKER AND THE KID

I called my broker and got a tip,
It shot up strong, then did a flip;
My, how quickly it fell, this bomb
And soon my money was all gone.

I dialed chat rooms and got a tip,
It shot up strong, then did a flip;
For where else go when Nasdaq booms,
Then to the net and stock chat rooms?

Sure enough, my broker's rich
From jerks like me, he's made commish;
That other sage, my chat room rater,
Turned out to be a smart sixth grader.

Henry Wadsworth Longfellow

ON DISAPPEARING FOOTPRINTS

THE TIDE RISES, THE TIDE FALLS

The tide rises, the tide falls,
The twilight darkens, the curlew calls;
Along the sea-sands damp and brown
The traveler hastens toward the town,
And the tide rises, the tide falls.

Darkness settles on roofs and walls,
But the sea, the sea in the darkness calls;
The little waves, with their soft, white hands,
Efface the footprints in the sands,
And the tide rises, the tide falls.

The morning breaks; the steeds in their stalls
Stamp and neigh, as the hostler calls;
The day returns, but nevermore
Returns the traveler to the shore,
And the tide rises, the tide falls.

THE DOW RISES, THE DOW FALLS

The Dow rises, the Dow falls,
You buy on margin, your broker calls;
Demanding money lest he dump
Your drooping holdings down the sump,
And the Dow rises, the Dow falls.

You chew your nails and walk the floor
Then overseas, the CAC[1] and FTSE[2] roar;
Some buying waves on Europe's bourses,
Erase with inter'est all your losses,
And the Dow rises, the Dow falls.

The new dawn breaks; a chance to grow rich
Comes by phone, in a peddler's pitch;
Your broker's back, he's cocky sure
His threats forgot you'll buy some more,
And the Dow rises, the Dow falls.

[1]The benchmark French stock exchange
[2]The benchmark United Kingdom stock exchange

John Greenleaf Whittier

MAUD MULLER (EXCERPT)

...of all the sad words of tongue or pen,
The saddest are these: "It might have been."

BLOWN CHANCES (EXCERPT)

...Of all the sad words you've heard in this boom,
The saddest were these: "I sold too soon!"

Edgar Allan Poe

ANNABEL LEE (ABRIDGED)

It was many and many a year ago,
In a kingdom by the sea,
That a maiden there lived whom you may know
By the name of Annabel Lee;
And this maiden she lived with no other thought
Than to love and be loved by me.

I was a child and she was a child,
In this kingdom by the sea,
But we loved with a love that was more than a love,
I and my Annabel Lee:
With a love that the winged seraphs of heaven
Coveted her and me.

And this was the reason that long ago,
In this kingdom by the sea,
A wind blew out of a cloud, chilling
My beautiful Annabel Lee;
So that her high-born kinsman came
And bore her away from me,
To shut her up in a sepulchre
In this kingdom by the sea.

Now the moon never beams, without bringing me dreams
Of the beautiful Annabel Lee;
And the stars never rise, but I feel the bright eyes
Of the beautiful Annabel Lee;
And so, all the night-tide, I lie down by the side
Of my darling, my darling, my life and my bride,
In the sepulchre there by the sea,
In her tomb by the sounding sea.

NEVERWASH SOX

I was many and many bucks ahead,
From my gambit owning stocks,
There was a start-up my savings I'd fed
By the name of Neverwash Sox;
And this company's shares just raced right ahead
Like a sprinter off of the blocks.

I was a novice and it had great promise,
This maiden voyage with stocks;
My chat room buddies took similar flyers
In burgeoning Neverwash Sox.
We tallied our windfalls and thought that we'd earned them
Like greedy Goldilocks.

Then for reasons sad, some government guys,
Took a step that cleaned our clocks,
The SEC said the books were cooked
And delisted my Neverwash Sox;
In one fell swoop our chat room group
Watched its profits blown away,
It came to us quite suddenly
That we should have bought eBay.

Now I tune out fast, a financial newscast
Lest it mention my Neverwash Sox;
And I feel great rage, when a business page
Has a story 'bout Neverwash Sox;
It's true, every night-time, I mourn this stock's decline,
Oh you start-up—my start-up—that made me feel fine,
When they flushed your remains out to sea,
Along went my buddies and me.

I DIED FOR BEAUTY

I died for beauty, and was scarce
Adjusted to the tomb,
When one who died for truth was lain
In an adjoining room.

He questioned softly why I failed?
"For beauty," I replied.
"And I for truth—the two of us are one;
We brethren are," he said.

And so, as kinsmen met a'night,
We talked between the rooms,
Until the moss had reached our lips,
And covered up our names.

I TANKED ON OPTIONS

I tanked on options, and sat there
Imbibing like a fool,
When one whose futures tanked plopped down
On an adjacent stool.

He muttered thickly, what's your grief?
"Call options," I soft sighed,
"Futures got me—the same damn things;
"We're suckers both,"he sobbed.

And so two losers drank all night,
We really got quite ripped,
Until the bar keep threw us out,
And counted up our tips.

Emily Dickinson

I NEVER SAW A MOOR

I never saw a Moor,
I never saw the sea;
Yet know I how the heather looks,
And what a wave must be.

I never spoke with God,
Nor visited in heaven;
Yet certain am I of the spot
As if the chart were given.

I NEVER MET AL GORE

I never met Al Gore,
I never heard George Bush;
But still I know that one's a bore,
And one just prattles mush.

I never felt the thud,
When markets find no bottom;
But daily tremors tip me off
That something here's gone rotten.

Walt Whitman

WHEN I HEARD THE LEARN'D ASTRONOMER

When I heard the learn'd astronomer;
When the proofs, the figures, were ranged in columns before me;
When I was shown the charts and the diagrams,
to add, divide, and measure them;
When I, sitting, heard the astronomer, where he lectured with
much applause in the lecture room,
How soon, unaccountably, I became tired and sick;
Till rising and gliding out, I wander'd off by myself,
In the mystical moist night-air, and from time to time,
Look'd up in perfect silence at the stars.

WHEN I SCHMOOZED THE TECHNICAL ANALYST

When I schmoozed the technical analyst;
When his lines, his patterns, were charted and placed before me;
When he explained support levels, and the theory of Fibonacci numbers;
When I, seated, with this furry-eared financial astrologer,
in a Wall Street tap room,
heard out his convoluted patter, I excused myself;
And promising to come again, I headed for the door,
Returned to my trading desk, where ever and always,
One sees a downturn and buys on the dip.

Walt Whitman

O CAPTAIN, MY CAPTAIN!

O Captain! my Captain! our fearful trip is done,
The ship has weathered every rack, the prize we sought is wcn.
The port is near, the bells I hear, the people all exulting,
While follow eyes the steady keel, the vessel grim and daring;
But O heart! heart! heart!
O the bleeding drops of red,
Where on the deck my captain lies,
Fallen cold and dead.

O Captain! my Captain! rise up and hear the bells;
Rise up, for you the flag is flung, for you the bugle trills,
For you bouquets and ribbon'd wreaths, for you the shores a-crowding,
For you they call, the swaying mass, their eager faces turning;
Here Captain, dear father!
This arm beneath your head!
Is it some dream that on the deck,
You've fallen cold and dead.

My Captain does not answer, his lips are pale and still;
My father does not feel my arm, he has no pulse nor will;
The ship is anchor'd safe and sound, its voyage closed and done,
From fearful trip the victor ship comes in with object won;
Exult O shores, and ring O bells!
But I with mournful tread,
Walk the deck my Captain lies,
Fallen cold and dead.

O EURO, MY EURO!

Oh Euro! My Euro! Your time has fin'lly come,
You've withstood all your critics flack, their doubting scoffs are done.
The franc's a ghost, the lira's toast, the deutschmark's just a mem'ry,
Around the globe thy name is hailed, in circles monetary;
But surprise! 'prise! 'prise!
You're still pris'ner of the Fed,
Because they keep the dollar strong,
Euros fall like lead.

O Euro! My Euro! rise up and take thy place;
Rise up, for you the guilder's gone, for you pesetas fled,
With you baguettes and schnitzels' bought, with you paella's ordered
No nation angst, no exchange rates, a Europe without borders;
Good Euro! hope bringer!
They promised you'd be sound!
So how come after all these months,
You've fallen 'gainst the pound.

The Euro keeps on dipping, it cannot find its legs,
This money has no value firm, it breaks through all the pegs;
The EU is a big success, it's quite the worldly hub,
In eastern lands they all aspire to join this happy club;
Exalt you Franks, and boast Teutons!
But I am far from sold,
While you play your Euro games,
Dollars I will hold.

Richard Hovey

THE SEA GYPSY

I am fevered with the sunset,
    I am fretful with the bay,
For the wander-thirst is on me
    And my soul is in Cathay.

There's a schooner in the offing,
    With her topsails shot with fire,
And my heart has gone aboard her
    For the Islands of Desire.

I must forth again tomorrow!
    With the sunset I must be
Hull down on the trail of rapture
    In the wonder of the sea.

THE MARKET DIPSY

I am hot to buy more Intel,
I am heavy in eBay,
For investing fever's got me
And it will not go away.

There's a tel.com just been issued,
Fiber optics hit the spot,
And I know this one can get me
To a place where rich folks squat.

So I must get in this action!
This new Intel I must buy
For a new econ'my's birthing
And I want my piece of pie.

Joyce Kilmer

TREES

I think that I shall never see
A poem as lovely as a tree.

A tree whose hungry mouth is pressed
Against the earth's sweet flowing breast;

A tree that looks at God all day,
And lifts her leafy arms to pray;

A tree that may in summer wear
A nest of robins in her hair;

Upon whose bosom snow has lain;
Who intimately lives with rain.

Poems are made by fools like me,
But only God can make a tree.

T's

I long for life that's worry free
So T-bills are the play for me.

A T whose payout is assured
When other debtors have demurred;

A T with coupons never lax
Because they're backed by income tax;

A T that gives a short-term edge
Unlike a note or long bond pledge;

It always beats inflation, too;
And it's so easy to renew.

Junk abounds that's triple-Cs[1],
But only Sam can issue T's.

[1]A bad junk bond rating

Index of Wall Street First Lines